Dear Ron,

Make your
mark

FIVE HIDDEN KEYS TO GREAT LEADERSHIP

May you make your mark!
All the best,

Steve

Steve Lawrence

Love you Ron!
Happy Birthday ☺
♡ Kathy

WP

Published by:
Wilkinson Publishing Pty Ltd
ACN 006 042 173
Level 4, 2 Collins St Melbourne, Victoria, Australia 3000
Ph: +61 3 9654 5446
www.wilkinsonpublishing.com.au

 A catalogue record for this book is available from the National Library of Australia

Make Your Mark — Five Hidden Keys to Great Leadership
Planned date of publication: 03-2019
Title: Make Your Mark — Five Hidden Keys to Great Leadership
ISBN(s): 978-1-925642-83-4: Printed — Paperback

Design: Michael Bannenberg
Printed and bound in Australia by Ligare

Contents

Foreword – John Kennedy Snr
(AFL Hall of Fame)

The subject of effective and efficient leadership continues to interest people and academics. Steve Lawrence's *Make Your Mark: Five Hidden Keys to Great Leadership* ought to be read and re-read by those concerned with the current paucity of inspiring leaders.

My association with Steve is through the Hawthorn Football Club which is conscious of its motto "Spectemur Agendo" (Let us be judged by our acts). Steve's career at the club shows him to be a man who not only "talks" but "does". His actions among his teammates on a club bus trip, a story told within the book, demonstrated his adherence to winning the personal battle as well as his courage in action. His life story of his own approach to leadership is factual and his personal integrity allows him to say that you lead for others and not for yourself.

For those who have been thrust into leadership positions there are risks which must be taken, as well as "stubborn adherence" to what is right. *Make Your Mark: Five Hidden Keys to Great Leadership* provokes thought and reflection.

Preface

My dad — Godfrey Lawrence — had three fathers, and yet it is only one whose influence has shaped my life.

Known as "Goofy", Godfrey Lawrence played Test cricket for South Africa and held the record for many years for the most wickets (28) in a Test Series (1961-2) by a South African bowler. For this feat he was awarded his country's prestigious Sportsman of the Year prize. Born in Rhodesia (Zimbabwe) in 1932, his father left his mother at a very early age. She later remarried a Victorian-era policeman whose cold, distant manner left my dad — the boy — feeling unloved and lost. At age thirteen, at the time of the conclusion of World War II, his beloved mother, Ira, died. Dad's life went into free fall. He was alone, without direction, without support and without love. Tall, gangly and now an orphan with almost no confidence, having missed much schooling in the years of his mother's illness, he was a vulnerable and hurting adolescent. Thanks to one man, however, things eventually turned around.

It was the presence, attention and belief of a teacher at the boarding school he was sent to, at the express wish of his mother in her will, who proved to be his truest "father". His biological father had disappeared, his step-father was distant and cold, but this man — Landreth — after whom one of my brothers is named, helped my dad to grow from boyhood to manhood. And he did this by being present to him and paying him authentic loving attention, investing in his future, and sharing the important values and beliefs that mark his life to this day. And he did it while teaching him how to play cricket.

I have learned from my dad, and through him from Father Landreth, many vital lessons of life, of manhood, and of success. These lessons have formed the foundation upon which are built the five hidden keys of great leadership I offer in this book. These include stories of my life as a professional footballer; as a husband and father of six children, having myself come from a broken family; of one who was a Director of Australia's largest ever event — the World Youth Day 2008 — as well as adventures of travelling the world, teaching and encountering extraordinary people. At times these include very painful personal struggles that I've lived through which, hopefully, illustrate the truth that important victories often emerge from failure and that strengths can be borne from weakness or personal wounds.

It is my hope that you, the reader, are inspired and equipped to be the great leader you exist to be, that you make your mark, and in your own particular situations you positively transform the people in your life and the cultures around you in such a way that produces an enduring impact for good.

MAKE YOUR MARK

Introduction: Leadership with Character

We face today a crisis of leadership.

In many ways the leadership we see in our political life and that of business is an expression of the crisis that exists in our culture. Our culture is often shallow, dysfunctional and morally confused; where human dignity is regularly undermined for the sake of convenience, and the human person reduced to a commodity, a consumer or mere functional mechanism. We need leaders with vision, great people who bring the greatness out in others. Above all, we need leaders with character.

Whenever we see a failure of leadership it is often a failure of character. Examples abound. The SS *Titanic* sank in 1912, not because of a lack of technical shipping knowledge and capability, but due to the bad decision made by its captain who gave in, against his better judgement, to ego-fuelled pressure imposed upon him by the ship's owner to arrive into New York early, thus pushing the ship to an excessive speed that prevented it from avoiding that iceberg. The "sub-prime crisis", which triggered the Global Financial Crisis of 2007-2008, was founded upon unscrupulous lending by banks such as Lehmann Brothers whose bankruptcy prompted the immediate plummeting of the market. Adolf Hitler was doubtless effective, efficient and highly organised in his attempt to restore and impose German national identity and to destroy the Jewish people, but there is also no doubt his leadership was a disaster because of his extraordinary and flagrant disregard for justice, which is the virtue of giving to people what is due to them. This book, in contrast to those instances of failure, presents examples of leaders with character. People who exhibited triumph over trials, people whose leadership has produced an enduring impact for good; these are the basis of this book.

Leadership and management are not the same thing, though they often depend on each other. Management is the art of getting things done. It is not the purpose of this book to write about management. Leadership, which is the focus of this book, is the art of making people and organisations grow, of enabling their most authentic selves, of transformation. Leadership is the exercise of virtuous character, where greatness of heart and humble service, together, permeate everything a person is and does. Leadership is as much about *who* a person is as *what* that person does. Some leaders are born, but even these need to be developed. Everyone can be a leader in their own way: in their families, in the workplace, in their communities. Great leaders have a clear sense of who they are, a strong vision of where they are going and a clear and determined sense of what they need to do to realise their purpose.

The mission at *Altum Leadership Group*, and with it this book, is to inspire and equip good leaders to become great leaders and in so doing transform the people and cultures around them to become great. "Altum" (Latin) means "High" and "Deep"; and so "Altum Leadership" is the vision of leadership that realises its high purpose and goes to the depths — both human and spiritual — of leaders, enabling them to be their greatest, most passionate and authentic selves. It seeks to help people overcome the obstacles preventing them from realising their purpose and to enable them to address the very concrete circumstances of their professional and personal lives, in ways that make a positive and enduring impact.

Make Your Mark: Five Hidden Keys to Great Leadership offers five essential keys every leader needs to exercise in order to open the doors to greatness. Each chapter follows the following method: one of the five keys is the focus of the chapter, starting with illustrious examples of great leadership from men or women in public life from recent or ancient history. Such examples are followed by the outline of the idea of a hidden key, developed with various considerations, both theoretical and practical, supported by an example or two from my own personal life experience. Each chapter concludes with questions to consider.

It is my hope to inspire and equip you, the reader, to grasp these keys to great leadership, use them on the locked doors you encounter, so as to make your mark and leave an enduring impact on our world.

Hidden Key #1

RISK WALKING
NEW PATHS

Imagining new possibilities

What is "hidden" about this key is the yet unseen path upon which these leaders set out!

Frenchman Francois Michelin, third generation of the Michelin family to run the Michelin tyre business, was both a mathematical engineer and a savvy entrepreneurial businessman, and he could see the potential for a technologically advanced radial tyre in the period after World War II. Opposing the conventional wisdom of the industry experts who stuck rigidly to the tried and true methods, he was not only the first to appreciate the possibilities of the new sophisticated tyre technology, he also combined his knowledge of the product with how to bring it to market. He created and launched the radial tyre in the 1950s, taking enormous risks to put innovative creativity ahead of the bottom line. Michelin accomplished success by utilising personal qualities required to convince a large corporation and industrial sector very much bound by tradition. In so doing he not only transformed his company but the entire industry, taking the Michelin company from tenth largest manufacturer of tyres in 1960 to first in 1989 with a twenty per cent market share that year. By then the name Michelin had long become synonymous with tyres. It is no surprise, therefore, some of the world's most respected car makers such as Porsche, have chosen to work side by side with Michelin.

Francois Michelin's firm belief in the power of engaging human imagination was a key to his success.

Grounded in reality

One day in 1946, thirty-six-year-old school teacher Agnes Gonxha Bojaxhui of Macedonia was on a train when she saw a man dying in the street. This was not an uncommon reality for the people of that city in West Bengal, India, but for her on that day, she somehow knew it was a moment of decision in her life that, if taken, would propel her in a completely new direction. She was not considering an abstract idea but facing a concrete reality. What would she do? She chose to attend to the man and provide him with as much dignity as she could muster for someone dying in the gutters. From this moment her purpose became clear and a new life was born, inspiring others to join her, including a handful of her former school students. The person the world has come to know as Mother Teresa of Calcutta walked through the door that life opened up on that day, responding to what she termed "a call within a call." It started an extraordinary movement of service to the poor that, by the time of her death in September 1997, had established almost 600 foundations in 123 countries, with nearly 4000 Missionaries of Charity collaborators, so inspiring was her example. She acted at the moment of decision and her life, as well as that of many others, was never the same again.

Which path to take?

How do we know when the opportunity that life presents is the one which we must take? How do we have confidence to take up what may appear from certain points of view to be a crazy decision? What criteria do we use to take that step which may alter the trajectory of our lives and even our ultimate destiny?

I have often heard these and similar questions when speaking to audiences and in coaching contexts over the years. Inspiring and equipping good people to become great is a personal mission that burns in my heart. A huge desire to help people find answers

to these questions for their own lives and those of
others is a passion of mine.

There is no formula, of course, when guiding
individuals or groups. Each person's background
and situation is unique, as are their desires, gifts and
talents. The task, therefore, of accompanying those
who seek guidance in helping them make momentous
decisions is one of enormous responsibility requiring
deep listening and perceptive attention. In the face
of such a task there is always a kind of extraordinary
wonder that one must hold in relation to the gift and
mystery of that individual life and its possibilities. It is
a mixture of archaeology, detective work and deep-
sea fishing.

Affirming the full freedom and authority of that
person to make their own decision is the first basic
disposition which must be held. There is no place
for preconceived judgments, coercion or any form of
manipulation. Reflecting their own story back to them
and helping them see when their heart rises and falls,
in the midst of various considerations is paramount. A
thorough addressing of the pros and cons is vital, as
is a consideration of elements which might be more
hidden from the person at the outset. These may
prove significant over the course of the reflection.

Ultimately all good decisions are accompanied by the experience of peace and joy, even those which are difficult, and that may knowingly eventuate in hardship. The fruitfulness or definitive effectiveness of these decisions often takes a long time to crystallise, and one cannot always be certain in an objective sense the decision is right. However, in addition to external confirmations, people often do have strong convictions, what might be described simply by words such as "I just knew I had to do it!" or "It feels like the right thing to do!"

Accidents do happen!

In 1985, as a fifteen-year-old teenager beginning my final two years of senior school in Brisbane, Australia, I decided out of a determination to secure a good final academic score, I would not play football that season, but rather use all my spare time to study. This was despite the fact that for the previous four years I had shown myself to be a very talented footballer, representing my state of Queensland with distinction. My coach Daryl was persistent in his efforts to get me to reconsider, yet even after the season proper had started, I held my ground. After time, however, I began to get 'itchy' to play. Being a sports-loving person, I found I was becoming more and more irritable without the thrill of competition, the camaraderie, and the satisfaction which comes from physical exertion in my life. I realised, too, the lack of balance in my activities was not helping my studies anyway! So, I willingly gave in to Daryl's insistence and played my first game with the Under 17 Mount Gravatt Australian football ("footy") team, without any training under my belt. It was the third game of the season.

That season just happened to be the one when the Hawthorn Football Club in Melbourne (one of the teams in the competition of the highest professional level of Australian football) came looking at me to recruit a future ruckman. This was a very unlikely scenario given the state of Queensland was still a "footy" backwater at that time, its winter dominated by the two rugby codes. Nevertheless, the city of Brisbane was being prepared to field a Queensland-based team in the emerging national competition, the Australian Football League, its first AFL game earmarked for 1987. So, in 1985, Hawthorn was getting in early so I could be recruited prior to the situation emerging where all Queenslanders would be zoned to its home Brisbane team for first selection options, ahead of the introduction of a draft system, which currently exists.

It was in August of that year, in the second half of the season, I was unknowingly being watched by Hawthorn's recruiting officer, John Hook, during a game where I happened to be the best player on the field. At the end of the contest he spoke with me about the prospect of signing a contract with the Hawks and so, for the first time in my life, I considered playing football in the Australian Football League. This extraordinary prospect is the dream of most young footy-loving Victorian boys from their earliest days and those of the other football states, predominantly South Australia and Western Australia. For me, the first time I ever thought of such a prospect was when I was asked to take it up! Life was presenting me with an opportunity and I knew in my bones that I just had to do it.

I finished high school at the end of 1986 and in January of 1987, with a one-year contract under my belt, I set out on an adventure that moved my life to Melbourne where I ended up playing twelve years for the Hawks (the animal emblem of Hawthorn), including in its 1991 victorious Premiership team where I was awarded the Player of the Finals series.

Melbourne was also where I met my beautiful wife Annie and where so many other wonderful offerings that life has presented to me have taken place. Considering I had originally decided not to even play football the year I was eventually recruited, it is striking how life's paths often open up so unexpectedly. I am certainly an accidental footy star!

A new stirring and a new risk

Currently, now 49 years of age, I am stepping out into a very new stage of my life, leaving aside a successful and secure career as an educational leader and teacher, taking the risk of starting up my new business Altum Leadership Group. Even though I have felt a stirring in my heart that has been telling me for some time to step out into this unknown territory of professional speaking, coaching and writing, there is still a significant element of daring which I, along with Annie, am taking in these steps. Time will tell how it proceeds, however, I feel confident (most days) and will give it everything I've got to succeed.

QUESTIONS TO CONSIDER

- *What stirring is there in your heart? What are you going to do about it?*

- *If you were to die today, what is that one thing you would regret you did not step out to do?*

- *What dreams buried inside of you require action for you to realise them?*

- *Are you playing it too safe?*
  Are you too busy?

- *What is one small action you can take to discover your purpose?*

- *Who is one person you can talk to, so as to help you gain greater insight into making your next step?*

Hidden Key #2

FIND GREAT COLLABORATORS

Great people make people great

The great Roman lawyer and statesman, Marcus Tullius Cicero, who served as Consul in the year 63BC, is considered one of Ancient Rome's greatest ever orators and writers. Yet it is to his loyal private secretary, Marcus Tullius Tiro, that we can attribute the credit of ensuring posterity has left us records of Cicero's speeches. Tiro's work has contributed extensively to the depth of our historical knowledge of both the political machinations which took place in the that led up to Julius Caesar's assassination, as well as the ensuing power struggle lead to the *Pax Romana* under Caesar Augustus, which reached its high point around the time of the birth of Jesus Christ.

The complementarity of these two men's gifts maximised the greatness of both of them in their public service: of Cicero who, as public speaker, articulated the needs of the people and the responsibilities of the state; and of Tiro who, as scribe to one of the great, penetrating and most industrious minds of the age, developed his own unique forms of shorthand writing which has come to us from across the centuries. Symbols such as "&" and abbreviations like "etc" are but two examples of about

4000 shorthand forms created by Tiro as he sought to record the brilliant words of Cicero the statesman. Great leaders find great collaborators which help both to succeed.

Our contemporary history is littered with examples of success stories which were impossible to achieve alone. Steve Jobs' Apple Company would never have succeeded without the technical brilliance of Steve Wozniak. Neil Armstrong would never have taken those first famous steps on the moon in July 1969 had Michael Collins, who in the end never walked on the moon, not been loyally circling in orbit in Apollo 11. Elton John's song writing partnership with Bernie Taupin is legendary.

Discovering complementarity

One of the key points of discernment I offer young couples considering getting engaged is to get each to ask, "Am I more myself when I'm with him/her?" In other words, to ask if this person is gifted in such a way — through their personality, temperament and character — that by uniting myself with them, my own gifts, strengths and qualities emerge even more than they would without them. In short, does he/she help me realise my purpose in life?

These questions presuppose the fact we need people to complement us so that the truest significance of our lives can be fulfilled. This is as true in life as it is in love. Great sporting teams know complementarity brings out the best in the team and that team balance with regard to types, body size, and skill-set is a key factor in its success. Collaborative partnerships are vital for all leaders, even if one individual takes greater public prominence. Edmund Hillary climbed Everest with the vital support of Sherpa Tenzing Norgay and Frodo successfully managed to break the power of the ring at Mount Doom in Tolkien's *Lord of the Rings* trilogy, only because of the loyal backing of his fellow halfling, Samwise Gamgee.

Building a new team

In 1996, when I was made Director of a city-wide ministry in Melbourne, I inherited a team who not only did not share my vision for the work but did not, in part, share the vision of the organisation. Despite my best efforts to bring the team along it became very clear from the outset I did not have the people

I needed to succeed in the job. Either I had to leave and go elsewhere, or they did.

With the support of my boss and the advice and guidance of a professional advisor I set out to restructure the organisation. Being young and inexperienced I did this more clumsily than I would have liked, but the eventual outcome was that people saw the writing on the wall and left, which afforded me the opportunity to start afresh. It took me two years to get to this point and in the space of a few months I was able to find two new collaborators, a man and a woman. They not only shared the broader vision of the organisation I sought to implement, they also provided vital qualities, contacts and ideas that I was able to adopt and lead with. It is not important that "I" don't have all the qualities required to do the work, but rather "we" have them. These two collaborators were both better than I was in a range of areas, but in our working together, through a profound mutual trust, we were formidable.

In fact, by the time I left the organisation in the year 2000, taking up an offer to run an international training school in Europe, the work we established together was thriving healthily, with many new positive projects and the vital engagement of growing numbers of people from a broad cross-section of our target group. What had previously been an inert and largely ineffectual operation had developed into a bouncing success. The unity of purpose of the small leadership team proved to be at the core of our effectiveness. This unity was by no means a uniformity, but rather a cohesive complementarity. The unity, harmony and creative openness so evident in all our interactions spilled over and proved to be a source of attraction and confidence for so many who entered into our orbit.

QUESTIONS TO CONSIDER

- *What are you not good at that requires you to find someone who is?*

- *What qualities, skills or abilities do you have that would be enhanced by suitable partnership with others?*

- *What dreams or ideas have you dropped because you lacked suitable support to bring them to fruition?*

- *What is the main obstacle you face in building a partnership?*

- *Who is one person you can speak to, so as to overcome that obstacle?*

Hidden Key #3

WIN THE INTERNAL BATTLE

Prisoner

I was born in South Africa when Nelson Mandela
was digging ditches as a prisoner on Robben Island.
My family — mum, dad and three brothers — left
the South Africa of Apartheid in December of 1973,
arriving by boat in Sydney in January 1974, a year
before Cyclone Tracey devastated Darwin. Mandela had
already been in prison for ten years when our Italian
ship, the Galileo Galilei, which I learnt later sank in
1999, disembarked for Australia from Cape Town. The
dock of Cape Town is 7km from Robben Island.

Mandela would spend 27 years as a political
prisoner. He was faced with the decision of how he
would respond to the realities of the injustice done
to him and to the lack of freedoms he experienced.
Mandela made the decision over time — day after
day after day — not to hate, not to resent. He knew
although most of his freedoms were denied him — he
couldn't decide for himself where to go, nor what to
do, nor what to eat, nor what to wear — but he could
decide what went on inside his heart.

Inspired by the *Invictus* poem of William Ernst
Henley (d. 1903), he set out to live by the phrase,
"I am the captain of my soul." He chose to forgive,

he chose to see the good in others. He could have been like the myriad of others incarcerated for long periods who are crushed in their hearts by anger, hatred, resentment, disappointment; hardened or poisoned by the evil and envy that they allow to make a home there.

A matter of the heart

When he was released from prison in 1990 under F.W. de Klerk and then shortly after became president of the new South Africa in 1994, he miraculously guided the post-Apartheid era away from what many expected would end up in civil war. It was a surprise there was not a slaughter. He almost singlehandedly brought unity between the whites and blacks in South Africa.

He made a point of insisting on reconciliation commissions being set up, with no retaliation and no recrimination, desiring the good for all, black and white. This immediate post-Apartheid era in South Africa was as it was because of the transformation inside his heart. Leadership, great leadership, is a matter of the internal transforming the external. Leadership is a matter of the heart.

The war effort

Winston Churchill's eventual triumph in galvanising
the British Parliament in its determination to oppose
Hitler militarily and unequivocally, as beautifully
portrayed in the film *Darkest Hour*, is another prime
example in politics of this hidden key. Not until this
was accomplished, a feat by no means guaranteed at
the time in the face of the block supporting Neville
Chamberlain's previously held appeasement position,
was the British war effort able to set its face like flint
and initiate what would eventually lead to the Allied
victory in 1945. Where diplomacy and dialogue are
often the best mechanisms for unity and peace, a
dogged uncompromising position in the face of
relentless evil is — at times — the order of the day
and the only way to true peace. Churchill won the
internal battle and hence the external victory was
secured.

The thoughts played out in the theatre of the
mind also lay the foundation for one's actions in
life. What we think is what we become. Even small
examples illustrate the point. Choosing to set your
alarm early so as to wake and finish an important

work task with a fresh mind sets the tone for the next day's activities. Indulging in lustful thoughts can be the seed that bears the deathly fruit of adulterous actions. The discipline of physical training, often achieved in the lonely moments on a track or in a gym, goes a long way in determining victorious successful outcomes on a field or in the arena. Fear of the view others have about us can paralyse us to inaction.

Blocked thinking

When I first arrived at the Hawthorn Football Club in January 1987 I was already two metres tall but, as a seventeen-year-old, still quite skinny and, at 78kg, very light. Having as my new teammates, the previous season's 1986 Premiership champions, I was very conscious of my rookie status and embarrassed by my lack of physical strength. In fact, when we worked out in the gym I was terrified to do chin-ups. I literally could not do even one properly! I didn't want this to be found out. So, I worked on my chin-ups only when the gym was emptied, which meant I hung around late to do them, if I did at all. My progress was slow, not surprisingly. It was my blocked thinking, based on fear, that prevented me from performing the suitable actions required of me.

Being an interstate recruit from Queensland I felt a strong pressure to succeed, as most of the players training with the team in the pre-season at that time were locals from Victoria. Interstaters usually had a high profile, and tended to be ready-made players, such as champion rover Johnny Platten from South Australia or my fellow Queenslander Jason Dunstall. My deficiencies as a junior player from a non-football state were very noticeable early on, and I felt something of a fraud having the title of an "interstate recruit".

In his desire to push me hard and develop me quickly Allan Jeans, our legendary coach, continually yelled at me throughout my first pre-season training period. "RUUUUUUUNNNN!!!!" "You've got the turning circle of the Queen Mary, son!!" I simply did not have the base of fitness to keep up. Each day we trained harder than I could sustain and knowing I was already giving my best, I simply tried to survive, feeling sure, however, that I would not last more than one season at Hawthorn. I regularly vomited during training in those first months and wondered if I could succeed.

Despite my lack of confidence, the club offered me a second season contract after what I thought was an otherwise unremarkable season in the Under 19s and Reserves. Surprisingly, during the pre-season training of that second season, 1988, I found myself running at the front of the group, keeping up with all the activities, and feeling stronger and fresh to perform my skills relatively well. My capacity had expanded way beyond my expectation, to the point I started the season so well in the Reserves that I was selected to play my first senior AFL game in Round 5, replacing the suspended champion Dermott Brereton at Centre Half Forward. Remarkably, I kicked five goals in my first match versus North Melbourne. It was my first taste of AFL success.

My determination to push on despite feeling I was not going to be able to accomplish the task at hand was an internal battle I had to win.

QUESTIONS TO CONSIDER

- *What internal battle are you facing that you need to win? How are you going to find victory?*

- *What is the one vice that seeks to destroy you, your marriage, or your family?*

- *What step do you need to take to attend to the matters of your interior life?*

- *Where, when and how do you ponder or record your deepest thoughts and feelings?*

- *Who do you regularly speak with to share and discuss your struggles, your hopes and your next steps?*

- *What is the one thing you need to do today, to set your life on the path of its truest purpose?*

Hidden Key #4

YOUR LIFE
IS NOT FOR YOU,
IT IS
FOR OTHERS

Bob Buford

In 1987, in his early forties, Bob Buford was the President and CEO of a tremendously successful television company based in Tyler, Texas (USA). His was a good and growing marriage with the blessing of a very talented and promising son. At forty-four, having experienced a period of "success panic" — wondering if there was more to life and asking the question "how much money is enough?" — his life was struck by the tragic drowning of his only son Ross, who had recently graduated from University and was already earning a great deal of money.

The shock of the 1987 loss became a catalyst for deeper reflection about the purpose of Bob's life and the realisation there are in fact two halves of life; the first, during which people are pushed to succeed, and the second, which should realise a person's significance.

Under the tutelage of Peter Drucker, the man considered the father of modern management, Bob Buford developed Halftime, a movement based on his book of the same name, helping people to move from success to significance, to "find their life purpose now." Buford's work emphasises, contrary to the accepted wisdom, that a person's second half, instead of being a period of slow decline, should in fact be better than the first, becoming the time where genuine legacy for others is enacted through the realisation of one's life mission.

In another's place

Maximilian Kolbe, Auschwitz prisoner number 11670, did the unthinkable.

In August 1941, ten men on an insufferably hot parade ground were being randomly chosen by the brutal Nazi Commandant Fritsch to go to their deaths in the starvation bunker, as both punishment and a future deterrent because of the escape of one prisoner. One of the ten chosen pleaded for mercy, being a married man with children. Kolbe stood out of line and risked violent retaliation. "I'll go in his place," he stated quietly and yet firmly. He had seen and heard the desperation of the fellow Pole, and whose weeping and pleading moved his heart. Despite not knowing the man personally, Kolbe proposed to replace him in the starvation bunker.

A lifetime of small acts

Such selflessness centred on the good of others, even to the point of one's own significant detriment or death, is not something which comes easily, nor does it simply emerge in an heroic moment. It is rather the effect of the culmination of a lifetime of such acts, beginning with small sacrifices and developing into virtuous habits of giving, habits that develop embedded character. Kolbe was known for that throughout his life, which was why he attracted so many to his cause in the years before the war, building up a thriving community of Franciscans, widely disseminating a highly effective publication and helping to provide refuge for 3000 Jewish refugees fleeing Nazi occupied Poland. His ultimate offering in Auschwitz became possible because of the numerous selfless offerings made daily.

Time, effort and talent

Many of the messages in our contemporary culture speak to us of the opposite idea, to put ourselves first. "Be comfortable". "Do what's easy, what feels good". "Go with the flow". How inspired are you by the lives of those who are selfish, greedy, lazy, "me first people"? How much is your heart raised up by their example?

Great leaders look around them and see what they can do to lift others up, they develop corporations not only to be successful financially, but to do good to others. They make time, exert effort and use their talents to empower and enable others to realise their purpose and mission in life, which inevitably continues the upward and outward spiral of positive culture building. Great leaders create families, of one sort or another, such as did Maximilian Kolbe, to bring love into the world. When there is not love in the world, these people don't complain, they respond by putting love in the world, and then it is found that there is love in the world. At the very moment he was arrested, prior to being taken to Auschwitz, his final words to his Franciscan brothers were "Forget not love!"

Healed people heal people

My teenage years were incredibly painful. From the time I was about twelve until I left home at the age of seventeen, my parents went through a period of incredible conflict, which eventuated in their separation, coinciding with the time of my move to Melbourne. There was no physical violence but the arguing that went on into the night, day after day, week after week, month after month, was completely unknown by my friends. It was a suffering I lived alone, and I couldn't even tell my best friend, whose house I often went to for refuge. Sometimes I went to sleep weeping. At times the agony was so great I would walk out the back door, stand in the middle of the back yard and yell at the top of my lungs an almighty "rooooaaaaaaarrrrr." The negative impact of their ongoing conflict continues in my emotions, my memories and reactions to this day.

After the disaster of my parents' separation I found it incredibly difficult to believe that marriage was possible and very much feared making the commitment to Annie, even though her love and constancy was a balm to my wounded soul. Over time I trusted that, despite my negative experience, I was not consigned to being a prisoner of my psychology. I desired a family and after finally developing the courage to take the step of marrying Annie, having wobbled a little for a few months, we married in 1992 and have developed a wonderful relationship which we share with many people. Since marrying, we have received the gift of six beautiful children, four of whom are now adults, all six wonderfully unique and special people.

A quote often used by a school principal I once worked for disturbed me. He said "wounded people wound people." And although this is clever, as well as quite true when wounds are allowed to fester without forgiveness, love and support, nevertheless it is also a limited truth. For it is also true that "healed people heal people," a statement which I believe is true of me. One of the great blessings of my life has been to help other married couples build good relationships and to avoid the many pitfalls I saw in my parents' marriage which I was determined to steer away from in my own marriage.

So, making our life a gift to others does not mean we need to come from perfect situations where we have it all in hand. Often time it is through incredible hardship and suffering of some sort or another that we discover an eventual avenue to a meaningful gift of our life for others. I would probably not be serving married couples had I not come from a situation such as I did. Our history can often determine our purpose.

What is important now?

Every day I apply the WIN formula to situations where I need to make a decision. The WIN formula means I ask "what's important now?" Thinking from the point of view of being on my death bed, should I do this or that? What's important now? It often helps me to choose to spend that little time with one of my children instead of doing that extra work, or to give a kind response when a mistake is made rather than getting angry, or to put some time of silence ahead of filling all my time with activity.

Great leaders do what is important now, they make their aim the love of others, and are not deterred even by the worst situations.

QUESTIONS TO CONSIDER

- *What small act of self-sacrifice will you do on a regular basis that benefits someone in your life?*

- *What kind of person do you want to become? How will you do it?*

- *In one challenge you are now facing, what is the important thing for you to give priority?*

- *How can you transform the suffering you have experienced into a gift for others?*

- *Is the focus of your life more about success or significance? In what ways do you search for significance?*

- *In what ways could your history illuminate your purpose?*

- *What is your personal mission in life?*

Hidden Key #5

DO WHAT IS
RIGHT
ALWAYS

The bus

When Rosa Parks refused to give up her seat on a bus on 1 December 1955 in Montgomery Alabama (USA), in defiance of the bus segregation laws, she acted as one individual "tired of giving in" to what undermined her human dignity. Her action famously provided impetus to the Civil Rights Movement in America, most notably championed by Martin Luther King Jr. Her defiance against what was a culturally established wrong was part of an ongoing struggle that cost her greatly, as it did King who was assassinated in 1968 to silence his inspiring effectiveness. The very sacrifices they were willing to make fuelled the momentum their opponents sought to oppose.

People Power Revolution

Corazon "Cory" Aquino, self-proclaimed "plain housewife" and mother of five children, was the spouse of Philippine Senator Benigno Aquino Jr, the staunchest critic of dictator President Ferdinand Marcos. Benigno was assassinated in 1983 and Cory was exiled to the USA. She returned from exile and ran for President in what were allegedly rigged elections where Marcos was proclaimed the winner. In defiance, she called for civil disobedience, gained support from armed forces and the local Catholic leadership, and thus led what came to be known as the "People Power Revolution" which, in 1986, toppled Marcos and brought her to the presidency.

As President in 1987 she amended the Constitution to limit the powers of the President, restored public confidence by emphasising civil liberties and a concern for human rights, as well as focussing upon the restoration of economic health, and resolving problems created by extremist polarising elements. She has become known as the "Mother of Asian Democracy".

Not unlike Mahatma Gandhi, who transformed his country during the Indian independence movement through peaceful civil disobedience, Cory Aquino did what was right despite the risks and murderous opposition. Goodness has its own power.

Private acts have public consequences

We live in a morally relativistic age, which means many people argue right and wrong are simply social constructs determined by circumstances, personal perspective and/or the perceived usefulness of acts on the basis of outcomes. Rosa Parks had no idea how effective her stand would be for others. Irrespective of the circumstances, one ought to always do what is right. And no matter how private, every act has a public dimension to it. The secret embezzlement of funds, for example, eventually makes its impact on shareholders. The broken promise of a father to his daughter adds one extra weight onto the scales of judgement she makes about whether authority in the world can be trusted. The ability of a spouse or partner to overcome pride and apologise for being wrong can shape not only both of their moods for that day, but can also bring down a wall that might otherwise eventually destroy the relationship.

Another bus

On one occasion when I was playing football with Hawthorn in 1994, the team boarded a bus for its annual pre-season training camp. I sat at the back of the bus among our fifty players, while the coaches and other officials headed off in their cars. After turning on the engine, before even exiting the car park, the bus driver began playing an X-rated pornographic video on the television. Even when averting my eyes to avoid looking, the sound effects left little to the imagination. It is almost impossible in our sexually saturated society for a young man not to be exposed to and thus wounded by, pornography, even with the most determined desire to avoid it. I had certainly seen it before and knew that I did not need such images running around in my mind at night.

Nervous... I wondered what to do

Many of my teammates at Hawthorn were among the most decorated and legendary players in the history of modern Australian football. There were also huge personalities in that group and although I had played in a Premiership in 1991, I was still quite shy of standing out from the crowd. But I knew I had to do something as the sounds of "ooh ahh" would presumably continue until the bus arrived at its destination two hours later. What was more awkward was my place on the bus. I was sitting in the very back seat, so should I do anything it would be impossible to be discreet. I stood up, without really knowing what I would do, and walked the length of the bus towards the front. As I did, still having no idea what action — if any — I would take, there started a growing chorus of "whhhhoooo" from the players in the bus. They would have seen that I was moving to the front and having previously taken a stand on a few moral issues, probably sensed I was going to make some form of protest. Football clubs can be wonderful places of camaraderie and collaborative efforts towards excellence, as ours was, but testosterone-fuelled mob rule can also kick in at times. As I approached the front, my knees feeling weak and my mouth dry from nervousness, with a raucous "wwwooooaaaahh" growing, I wondered what to do.

A valuable lesson

Just before arriving at the bus driver, in what seemed a very long march to the front, I noticed the player sitting immediately behind the bus driver and remembered that he was only seventeen. So, I leaned down and quietly said into the bus driver's ear, "You have a minor on board this bus. What you are doing is illegal. Turn it off." Without looking around and without hesitation, he reached up and switched off the television. That was the easy part, because now I had to turn and face the players and the music! If the walk to the front was long, the return walk to the back would be longer. So, I turned and went back to my seat. Something amazing then happened, which taught me a valuable lesson, one I have never forgotten. No one said a thing to me! Not then, not throughout the bus trip, not even on the weekend training camp. In fact, no one raised it with me that whole season, nor did anyone ever even hint at it for the remainder of my football career! Over time I assumed it was an episode forgotten, but it taught me that sometimes even in the face of total opposition and especially when we can feel very weak and even uncertain, we can sometimes win the day simply because doing what is right has its own power.

A lesson on leadership

There is an important addendum to this story, which took place more than seventeen years after the bus incident. On the day of the 2011 funeral of our legendary Hawthorn coach Allan Jeans, one of the greatest AFL coaches of all time, I was having coffee with two of my Premiership teammates. One of them,

Andy Collins, said to me, "Do you remember the time you got the porno turned off on the bus to Phillip Island?" It was the first time it had ever been raised with me for nearly eighteen years! "Yes" I smiled. Darrin Pritchard also recalled it. "Well," he went on, "as you know I've been a senior coach in South Australia and one of my duties has been to travel all over the state speaking with thousands of young people. I want you to know that wherever I go I tell that story of what happened in the bus, and when I do," he continued, "I tell them I think it is the greatest act of leadership I'd ever seen." I'm not sure if I would agree with his conclusion but this is what he certainly said to me. "That is because you knew everybody disagreed with you but you still did what was right."

I was struck by his recount, partly because the event had not been lost, partly because no-one had ever mentioned to me they had heard the story, but also because of how public the action had been made. Here was I thinking it had been forgotten. What struck me was how, even without realising it, our actions have far reaching implications and our leadership, often in those accidental moments of conflict and testing, is brought to light in ways we can never know or manufacture.

QUESTIONS TO CONSIDER

- *Consider one situation where you have been in a conflict between your values and the expectations of those around you. Did you live up to your values?*

- *What is one obstacle preventing you from doing what is right at all times? How can you overcome it?*

- *What price are you willing to pay for integrity?*

- *How do you sharpen your conscience? What else can you do?*

- *Who can help you to gain clarity where you have confusion?*

- *Who are the people in your life who most need your moral leadership?*

Conclusion

I would like to conclude this book on greatness in leadership with a paradox about the "great" importance of "small" things, illustrated by beavers. Beavers, what they call in America "little critters", build dams with many small sticks. Tiny little twigs, not very significant, one would imagine. And yet, piled up, one on top of the other, a dam is constructed, so that the whole flow of the river is blocked! This can be like our relationships. Most failed relationships – whether in marriage, in the workplace, among siblings, or between friends – don't tend to fall apart simply as a result of one major problematic event or action. Sometimes, it is true, this can be the case, but mostly not. Mostly, it is because a multitude of little things we do wrong to each other, or actions we don't take that we ought to, pile up like those many little sticks gathered by our friend the beaver, and all of a sudden there is a huge block or a wall between us.

It is really important, therefore, that for all of our key relationships we establish a platform for the quick, regular and easy enabling of forgiveness. As the saying goes, one that Annie and I try to live by, "Don't let the sun go down on your anger." This is not easy, but vital that we constantly clear away those sticks that build up. We need, for the sake of healthy relationships, to learn how to say sorry well and how to forgive well.

And in our times, there seems to have emerged in public life a professional way of apologising, which, while not articulated this way often amounts to something akin to "I'm sorry … we got caught!" It does not take responsibility for actions. We need, rather, when we have wronged another to admit our fault and say "I'm sorry. I shouldn't have done that. It was wrong." And even if there are factors which mitigate against our culpability, we still need to articulate that what we did was wrong. For example, and I quote a real situation from this week, "I'm sorry Annie for being a little rude a few times this weekend when I spoke to you. I shouldn't have done that. I was under pressure all week and was very tired because of it, but it was wrong of me to speak to you like that." Personally, I find it much easier to forgive when a person tells me the way they were wrong.

How we respond to that apology is also important. If we say, "Oh it was nothing" we diminish the gift of the apology. It was not nothing! Or, if we say, "That's okay" – well, its not okay to do what's wrong! We need to take seriously what we are communicating in such moments. If we say such things we may well be telling the person not to bother with apologising next time. I think, rather, we ought to say, "I forgive you." This way we are, first, honouring the apology, because, as we all know, it often takes some courage to ask forgiveness by admitting fault. Second, it acknowledges that what has been done was indeed wrong and ought not to have been done. And third, it clearly absolves the person from their wrong and is therefore much easier to put aside for the person doing the forgiving. "Forgiven, done. Let's now move on." When such clear dealing with a matter does not take place, in my experience, people tend to refer back to the events months and even years later, "Remember when you said…" as the resolution clearly did not happen. The sticks kept piling up.

Let's learn from the beaver, and make sure that the sticks are not building a dam that can destroy our relationships. Let's make forgiveness a regular, quick and easy aspect of our relationships, and let's learn to be good at it. Greatness in leadership depends on it.

The paradox I referred to at the beginning of this conclusion, then, speaks of how greatness is realised in smallness. To illustrate this point, I will entrust the final words of this book to the wise wizard Gandalf, from advice he gave to the hobbit Bilbo Baggins, advice we would all do well to heed: "Some believe it is only great power that can hold evil in check, but that is not what I have found. It is the small everyday deeds of ordinary folk that keep the darkness at bay. Small acts of kindness and love."

Acknowledgements

As this book is brief so too will be the acknowledgements, though in many regards there are so many people I wish to thank for their help. I will limit myself to a few. John Sikkema and Glenn Williams literally have been my saving grace during the transition period from my teaching time to the new adventure upon which I have recently embarked, John as a wise strategic and practical support, and Glenn for his encouraging, insightful and illuminating wisdom within the context of my own Halftime roundtable. It was during this transition that I wrote *Make Your Mark* and I am also grateful to John for helpful comments upon reading the manuscript.

Clent Jewell was to me in the reading of this manuscript what his surname suggests, and he offered many little pointers to improve both my thinking around who the audience might be and how they would read it, in addition to his helpful stylistic suggestions.

My brother, David Lawrence, himself an accomplished author with a range of fictional works under his belt, provided excellent perspective and suggestions, including courageously honest advice that only a brother can give. His fraternal scrutiny has challenged me and only helped to make the text more authentic.

Mark Wolfenden needs to be given the credit for articulating to me one of the five hidden keys found in this book, that of great leaders requiring great collaborators. I'm sure all the other keys have come to me in various ways and forms through a range of means and that none of them is actually original, nevertheless I do recall Mark specifically advising me on that one. The more I thought about it the more I knew he was right. He even provided me with a couple of the minor examples found in the text.

Thanks to my wonderful friends Therese Nichols, Founder and Director of One Plate, for her encouragement and recommendation, Alex Leach for his insightful and humbly worded comments, Dale Stevens for her dramatic insights, and Peter Muling for his suggestions.

Thanks also to Georgie for taking the cover photo, Jerome for his assistance in conceiving the concept of the cover design, Dom for the sharp eye he put to the final proofread, and to Therese de la Rose for her special assistance. Many thanks to Jeff Kennett for his recommendation of this work to

Michael Wilkinson, and for Michael's heartfelt and enthusiastic desire to publish. Thanks also must go to Michael Bannenberg for his creative work in the design of the cover and the interior of the book, and his special trick creating a new font for the title.

Thanks to Michael Arnot of *Encore Speakers* who helped me find a title for the book that would also encapsulate the title of a keynote address. Hence, he proposed *Make Your Mark*, which I've accepted in favour of the original title *Enduring Impact*. I had to detach myself from the original title but I soon realised that *Make Your Mark* is simpler and more directive and therefore activating in its language.

And last but certainly not least, I wish to thank my beautiful wife Annie for the 25 years of marriage that we recently celebrated. Had she not been in my life I'm certain that I would be much less than half the man that I currently am. Her father recently said to me, referring to our marriage, "The best thing you ever did!" He is absolutely correct in that, for she is without doubt the greatest created gift ever given to me.

My Next Book:
The Tiny Book for Giant Men

If you liked *Make Your Mark: Five Hidden Keys to Great Leadership* you may want to read my next book, *The Tiny Book for Giant Men*. All men are very conscious of their own limitation and struggles, and deep down feel their own inadequacy, tending to hide this from others. As a result, they believe the lie that they could never be great. Not so!

In *The Tiny Book for Giant Men* I tackle the very specific challenges men face in our world today and provide examples from my life and others to show how every man can become great, even if he sees his life as a disaster. Rather than succumbing to the advertising mantra which bombards men from every side asserting that "all men are useless", and against the often-relentless negativity that comes from within which speaks meaninglessness and futility to every man, I put to men the much-needed message: "You DO have what it takes!"

Whilst this book is primarily geared to men themselves, it includes an important acknowledgement on the vital and irreplaceable role women have in helping boys become men and ordinary men to become great. Certainly, it is very true it is men who need to speak and act so as to raise up the man from the boy, and I do recount many instances where this has taken place in my own life. My experience — however — also attests to key moments where women have spoken and acted to help me realise my purpose as a man. On one such occasion, as I was floundering in my responsibility of running an event, Martine, one of the leading women present, put her hands on each of the sides of my shoulders, looked up at me and smiled encouragingly, and said "You are a man!" — as if that explained everything! Something extraordinary happened to me in that moment as she helped me take my place, and to believe I wasn't in competition but in partnership, which is one of the gifts women offer men. In the context of that event I have always felt confident and capable. Annie too has had this influence on me.

It is, however, the influence of great men in my life who have primarily shaped and guided me, challenged and encouraged me, and inspired and equipped me to embrace the adventure of manhood. Stories of these men, both personally known by me as well as public figures whose example and words have provided vision and illumination from afar, offer rich material within the book that will help to unlock the greatness in every man.

Further Contact

For those who wish to make contact with me to explore speaking or coaching bookings, leadership training seminars or interviews, they can do so via my email at *Altum Leadership Group*:

steve.lawrence@altumgroup.net

or through my website:

http://altumgroup.net

or through my LinkedIn page:

https://www.linkedin.com/in/stephen-lawrence/

Further Reading

I have leaned on the following books quite heavily in my own personal and professional reading, and so I highly recommend them to you.

Bob Buford, *Halftime. Moving from Success to Significance*, Grand Rapids Michigan, Zondervan, 2008.

Andre Frossard, *Forget Not Love. The Passion of Maximilian Kolbe*, San Francisco, Ignatius Press, 1987.

Robert Harris, *Dictator*, Hutchinson, London, 2015.

Alexandre Havard, *Virtuous Leadership. An Agenda for Personal Excellence*, United States of America, Sceptre, 2007.

Alexandre Havard, *Created for Greatness. The Power of Magnanimity*, Bloomington Indiana, AuthorHouse, 2011.

Anthony Howard, *Humanise. Why Human-Centred Leadership is the Key to the 21st Century*, Milton Queensland, John Wiley and Sons, 2015.

Nelson Mandela, *Long Walk to Freedom*, Little, Brown Book Group, London, 2013.

Michael D. O'Brien, *Father Elijah*, Ignatius Press, San Francisco, 1996.

J.R.R. Tolkien, *The Hobbit*, Allen and Unwin: London, 1937.

J.R.R. Tolkien, *The Lord of the Rings*, HarperCollins, London, 2007.